When Parents Separate

Questions and Feelings About ...

W
FRANKLIN WATTS
LONDON•SYDNEY

by Dawn Hewitt

Illustrated by Ximena Jeria

Franklin Watts
First published in Great Britain in 2017 by The Watts Publishing Group

Credits
Editor: Melanie Palmer
Design: Lisa Peacock
Consultants and author: CHUMS / Dawn Hewitt CEO of CHUMS

CHUMS is a mental health and emotional wellbeing service
for children, young people and their families. The team
consists of experts in psychology, social work, play and
drama therapy and experienced practitioners who
regularly provide support, consultation and training.

ISBN: 978 1 4451 5656 9 (hbk)
ISBN: 978 1 4451 5657 6 (pbk)

Printed in China

MIX
Paper from
responsible sources
FSC® C104740
FSC
www.fsc.org

Franklin Watts
An imprint of
Hachette Children's Group
Part of The Watts Publishing Group
Carmelite House
50 Victoria Embankment
London EC4Y 0DZ

An Hachette UK Company
www.hachette.co.uk

www.franklinwatts.co.uk

COMHAIRLE CHONTAE ÁTHA CLIATH THEAS

SOUTH DUBLIN COUNTY LIBRARIES

COUNTY LIBRARY, TOWN CENTRE, TALLAGHT
TO RENEW ANY ITEM TEL: 462 0073
OR ONLINE AT www.southdublinlibraries.ie

Items should be returned on or before the last date below. Fines,
as displayed in the Library, will be charged on overdue items.

When Parents Separate

Children often live in a family which may include a mum, dad, brothers and sisters.

Every family is different.

Who is in your family?
Who do you live with?

Living in one house together
with both parents
is common.

But sometimes a mum might live in one house
and a dad in another. This happens a lot, too.

When families live in one house it can feel safe and you may feel happy. But your mum and dad may not be happy or be getting on with each other.

It is not unusual for people to argue. You may argue with your mum or dad sometimes.

You usually say sorry and forget about it later.

There are lots of reasons why parents may argue.
It can be hard to understand what is happening.
Sometimes parents argue
because of problems or
difficulties they may
have at work.

This may make them unhappy or bad tempered.
They may spend less time at home.

When parents are unhappy they may start behaving differently. They might get in a bad mood or not talk to each other.

Some parents may be upset or argue all the time.
It can make you feel upset, too.

How do you feel if you hear an argument at home?

Sometimes parents may not be able to solve their difficulties. They may decide that they cannot live together anymore. This is called separating.

This does not mean that they have stopped loving you, but they may not love each other anymore.

It can be hard to understand why parents have to separate. As well as feeling sad, you may also feel angry.

You might blame your parents for not trying hard enough to stay together.

Life at home can be difficult when your parents are in the process of separating.

Parents may say unkind things about each other because they feel hurt or upset.

They may not realise how this makes you feel.
It can be helpful to tell them, if you can.

*What have you felt
upset about?*

When parents separate it means one parent will move out to a new home. Or both parents may need to move to new homes. This change can be hard at first. It is normal to feel scared.

You might think it is somehow your fault,
or that you could have helped fix things.
But it isn't. Some problems are too big
to mend. People can change how they
feel about each other.

You may feel worried about who you are going to live with. But you will live with both parents at different times and have two bedrooms.

You will still have a
mum and dad, even if
they live apart.

Remember it is helpful to talk to someone else about how you feel, perhaps another family member or a teacher. There are many people who can help you.

Who would you talk to?

In the future a parent may find a new partner or marry someone else. You may have a bigger family with new brothers or sisters.

How would you feel about having more people in your family ?

It can take a long time to adjust to changes in family life. You may worry about ever feeling happy. However, you will notice that you adjust to living differently and life is okay again.

Things you can do

1. Draw a feeling body: first draw an outline of your body, then colour in the places in your body where you feel angry, sad, confused, lonely, worried etc. Try and talk to someone about them.

2. Make a collage: use a piece of card and cut out pictures in magazines that remind you of happy times with your family.

3. Make a coping pot: draw a pot and when you are worried or anxious write some words in it. You could show an adult or a teacher so that they can help you.

4. Use a support network : draw around your hand and on each finger and your thumb write the name of someone you can talk to or who cares for you.

Notes for parents and teachers

This book can be a useful guide for families and professionals to discuss divorce or separation, to aid communication in the family and to help promote discussion, enabling children to express their thoughts and feelings in a safe environment.

When parents split up it can be overwhelming for both them and their children. Within a family everything changes. Parents may find it helpful to be able to come to a shared decision on the story of why they are separating. Honesty is important and, over time, it may be more appropriate to share more but children deserve to have positive relationship with both parents.

Divorce and separation can cause grief reactions in both children and parents. This can include wider family and friends as well. Children may have lots of questions that will need simple answers. They may show they are upset in a variety of ways. They may become withdrawn or act out their feelings through their behaviour, becoming angry and challenging. They may become more clingy, tearful and anxious and blame themselves in some way. They might even be relieved.

It can be hard to support a child through a difficult transition. They need to spend time with each parent and routines and boundaries should be maintained as much as possible. This helps children to feel safe. Children need to have the opportunity to be listened to, to tell their story and to understand that what they are feeling is normal. Schools may be best placed to facilitate this. Lots of consistent messages need to be given and lots of extra cuddles and affection.

If you are separating it can be exhausting. It may be helpful to access some support for yourself. The more you look after yourself, the more you will be able to help your children. It can be a difficult journey but there is hope for a brighter future.

Further Information

Books

Dealing with ... My Parents' Divorce by *Jane Lacey and Venitia Dean* (Franklin Watts, 2017)
Mum and Dad Glue by Kes Gray and Lee Wildish (Hodder Children's, 2010)
My Family's Changing: A First Look at Family Break Up by *Pat Thomas and Lesley Harker* (Wayland, 1998)
Two Homes by Claire Masurel and Kady MacDonald Denton *(Walker, 2002)*

Websites

http://www.partnershipforchildren.org.uk
https://gingerbread.org.uk/content/separation-advice
https://www.kidsinthemiddle.org/
www.chums.uk.com